Quiz: 102742

Level: 3.5

Points: 0.5

WASHINGTON IS BURNING

BY MARTY RHODES FIGLEY

ILLUSTRATIONS BY
CRAIG ORBACK

M Millbrook Press/Minneapolis

The illustrator would like to thank the models who were used for the oil paintings, most especially Deonté Daniels as Paul Jennings, Susie Daniels as Sukey, and Jessica Silks for modeling and for her help with photography.

The photograph on p. 47 appears courtesy of the White House Historical Association, The White House Collection.

Text copyright © 2006 by Marty Rhodes Figley
Illustrations copyright © 2006 by Craig Orback

All rights reserved. International copyright secured. No part of this book may be reproduced, stored in a retrieval system, or transmitted in any form or by any means--electronic, mechanical, photocopying, recording, or otherwise--without the prior written permission of Lerner Publishing Group, except for the inclusion of brief quotations in an acknowledged review.

Millbrook Press
A division of Lerner Publishing Group
241 First Avenue North
Minneapolis, MN 55401 U.S.A.

Website address: www.lernerbooks.com

Library of Congress Cataloging-in-Publication Data

Figley, Marty Rhodes, 1948-
   Washington is burning / by Marty Rhodes Figley ; illustrations by Craig Orback.
      p.   cm. — (On my own history)
   ISBN-13: 978-1-57505-875-7 (lib. bdg. : alk. paper)
   ISBN-10: 1-57505-875-8 (lib. bdg. : alk. paper)
   1. Jennings, Paul, b. 1799—Juvenile literature. 2. Washington (D.C.)—History—Capture by the British, 1814—Juvenile literature. 3. United States—History—War of 1812—Biography—Juvenile literature. 4. Child slaves—Washington (D.C.)—Biography—Juvenile literature. 5. Slaves—Washington (D.C.)—Biography—Juvenile literature. 6. African Americans—Washington (D.C.)—Biography—Juvenile literature. 7. African American boys—Washington (D.C.)—Biography—Juvenile literature. 8. Madison, Dolley, 1768–1849—Juvenile literature. I. Orback, Craig, ill. II. Title. III. Series.
   E356.W3F45 2006
   973.5'2'092–dc22   2005011933

Manufactured in the United States of America
1 2 3 4 5 6 – JR – 11 10 09 08 07 06

For my brother Robert
—MRF

To Dale Jowsey for making me feel at home
—CSO

Monday morning, August 22, 1814
Washington City

Fifteen-year-old Paul Jennings
held the bridle.
President James Madison
mounted his horse.
The president was going to join the
American troops.
Thousands of British soldiers were
marching toward Washington City.
The American army had to stop them.
But many of the American soldiers
were new.
They were not ready to fight.

President Madison looked worried.
"Paul, I know I can depend on you
to help Mrs. Madison," he said.
"She has promised to stay here
and wait for me."
"I will do my best," said Paul.
Paul Jennings was a slave.
He was born on the Madisons'
plantation in Virginia.
James Madison became president of
the United States when Paul was nine.
Paul came to live in the President's House
in the capital city of Washington.

The President's House was a
grand white mansion.
It was the largest home in the country.
Paul was President Madison's
personal servant.

Paul watched the president ride away.

Then he returned to the house.

He went to the dining room

and looked up at a large painting.

It showed George Washington

standing tall and proud.

The first president of the United States

was dressed in black.

He was holding a sword.

Paul thought President Washington

looked just like a great leader should.

"Admiring George, are you?" a voice asked.

French John, the head servant,
stood behind Paul.

"George Washington won the
Revolutionary War against Britain,"
said Paul.

"Can we defeat the British again?"

America had been at war with Britain since 1812.

The war started because the British would not respect the United States.

The British stopped American ships at sea and took away American men.

They forced them to work on British ships.

French John shook his head in disgust.

"The secretary of war, General John Armstrong, is a fool.

He said the British would not attack Washington City.

Because of him, our troops aren't ready. Now the British are coming."

Paul looked out the window.
It had not rained in three weeks.
The city's streets were hot and dusty.
And they were jammed
with wagons and carriages.
Families were fleeing the city
with everything they could carry.

Paul wondered what would happen.

What if the American troops were defeated?

What if the British invaded Washington City?

Paul wished he could play his violin.

Making music always comforted him.

But there was no time now.

There was much to be done.

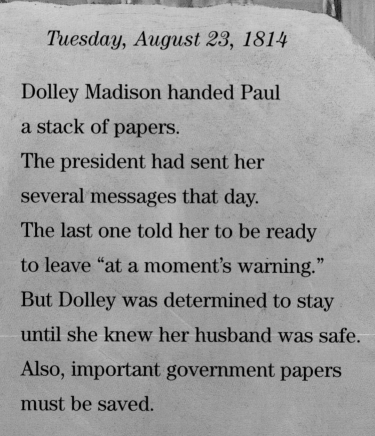

Tuesday, August 23, 1814

Dolley Madison handed Paul
a stack of papers.
The president had sent her
several messages that day.
The last one told her to be ready
to leave "at a moment's warning."
But Dolley was determined to stay
until she knew her husband was safe.
Also, important government papers
must be saved.

"Try to fit them in that trunk
before we latch it shut," she said.
Dolley's eyes twinkled.
"Anything we don't take with us,
the British will certainly steal!"

French John stomped into the room.

"The troops guarding the house
have run away!" he said.

"Cowards!" said Paul.

Everyone was escaping the city.

Paul tried to look brave.

But he didn't feel brave at all.

Dolley lifted her chin.

"Don't worry," she said.

"I have no fear for myself."

French John waved his fist angrily.

"I'll lay a train of gunpowder.

We can blow up the enemy if they
dare try to enter this house!"

Dolley patted him on the shoulder.

"That's not my way," she said.

Paul carried the trunk outside.

He put it in the carriage.

The streets were even more crowded

and noisy than before.

Back inside, the President's House was quiet.

The yellow walls of the parlor

glowed in the afternoon sunlight.

Rich red velvet curtains framed

the drawing room windows.

Silver lamps sparkled on the walls.

Each week, Mrs. Madison invited

both rich and poor people to these rooms.

She had a kind word

for everyone she met.

Now Mrs. Madison was in danger.

But she was not afraid.

Paul knew what he had to do.
He would help the president
and Mrs. Madison any way he could.
And he would stay brave and calm
no matter what happened.

Wednesday afternoon, August 24, 1814

Paul found Dolley upstairs.

She was moving from window to window,

looking through her spyglass.

Cannons rumbled in the distance.

A battle had begun six miles away

at Bladensburg.

"I see no sign of my husband's return,"

she said.

Dolley took a deep breath.

"No matter.

I will stay here until I know

my husband is safe."

The mayor of Washington City
had visited Dolley twice that morning.
He wanted her to leave the city.
She refused.

Paul saw that Dolley was worried.

What could he do to help?

"Shall I prepare for dinner?" he asked.

Mrs. Madison nodded.

"Yes, Paul," she said.

"We will have dinner at three as usual.

We will hope the battle will be won.

We will hope my husband will be here."

Paul set the dining room table
with the china with gold rims.
He cooled cider and wine.
Loud cannon booms rattled the windows.
But Paul calmly finished his task.

It was nearly three o'clock.

Mrs. Madison's maid Sukey

leaned out a window.

"Here comes James!" she yelled.

James Smith galloped toward the house.

He had ridden to the battle

with the president.

"The president isn't with him!"

said Sukey.

"Our cause is lost!"

Paul tried to comfort Sukey.

"Don't be afraid," he said.

James waved his hat.

"Clear out! Clear out!" he yelled.

"General Armstrong has ordered
a retreat!"

James carried a note from the president.

"My husband has sent word.

The battle has been lost," said Dolley.

"We must leave before the British arrive!"

Dolley looked one last time at the beautiful

rooms around her.

In the dining room, she stopped at the table.

"The British might eat our food," she said.

"But they will not have our silver!"

Paul helped Dolley put the silver in her bag.

Then Dolley looked up at the painting
of George Washington.
There was one more thing they had to do.
"Save that picture if possible," she said.
"If not possible, destroy it.
Under no circumstances allow it
to fall into the hands of the British!"

Paul and another servant found a ladder.

Paul tried to take down the picture.

But it was screwed tight to the wall.

French John handed Paul an ax

to break the frame.

Paul didn't want to use the ax.

He was afraid he would hurt the painting.

Dolley seemed to understand.

She told Paul to climb down

and hold the ladder for French John.

Finally, the picture was removed

from the frame.

Paul sighed.

George Washington's picture was safe.

Mrs. Madison, Sukey, and the coachman
drove off in the carriage.

On the streets, Paul watched frightened
people run in all directions.

Tears filled his eyes.

America's capital would soon be
in British hands.

Sundown, Wednesday, August 24, 1814

Paul walked to the Potomac River.

There he found the president and his men.

They were safe.

Together they waited for the ferry.

Paul did not know what would happen
to Washington City.

He felt his knapsack.

At least he had saved his violin.

The ferry took them across the river,
away from the city.
On the other side, wagons
full of soldiers passed them.
Some of the soldiers were white.
Some of the soldiers were black.
"They are Commander Barney's troops,"
said President Madison.
"They fought well at Bladensburg.
While others ran away,
they stood their ground."

Paul raised his hand in a salute.

One of the black soldiers
saluted back.

Paul felt proud of the brave black soldiers.

The president and his men traveled along
the shore of the river.

Paul looked back toward the city.

The sun had set, but the sky was glowing.

Washington was burning!

The British had set America's capital on fire.

Flames leaped in the air.

Paul had never seen such a terrible sight.

Sunday, August 28, 1814

Four days later, Paul returned to
Washington City with the president.
A storm had come while the
fires were burning.
A tornado hit the city.
The British soldiers had fled.
The rains from the storm helped
put out the blazes.
But the tornado had battered the city.

Huge trees were pulled up.
Roofs were blown away.
Most of the grand buildings
were burned-out shells.

Paul walked among the ruins of the
President's House.
The air smelled like smoke.
His beautiful home was destroyed.
Paul ran his hand over a white pillar.
It lay broken and cracked on the ground.
President Madison tried to comfort
people on the street.

"We will not let the British beat us!
We will rebuild the city!" he said.
Paul knew the president wouldn't
let the American people be chased away
from Washington City.
This battle was over.
But Paul wondered if the war
would ever end.

Wednesday, September 14, 1814

Paul sat on a window seat after dinner.
The Madisons had dined with
Dolley's sister and her husband.
Paul missed his home.
No one could live in the
President's House.
Only blackened walls
and ashes were left.

Paul stared out the window.
Carts filled with rubble clanked
down the Washington City streets.

French John rushed into the room.

"Good news, Paul," he said.

"There has been a grand battle at

Fort McHenry near Baltimore!

Our troops stood firm.

Our flag still waves!

The British didn't capture the fort!"

Paul was filled with hope.

He knew the Americans wouldn't give up.

Someday, the President's House

would be grand again.

George Washington's portrait

would hang on the wall again.

America would win its second war

for independence from Britain.

Paul Jennings began to play his violin.

His music drifted out the window

and up to the stars.

Afterword

Paul Jennings played his violin again on February 17, 1817, when President Madison signed the peace treaty with Britain.

The Americans rebuilt their capital city, but Paul Jennings and the Madisons never did return to live in the President's House. The repairs were not completed until James Monroe became president in 1817. The portrait of George Washington was hung once again in the President's House.

Paul Jennings served James Madison until the president's death in 1836. Lacking money, Dolley sold Paul in 1846. Soon after, at the age of 48, Paul was able to buy his own freedom.

In 1848, Paul helped plan a major slave escape. More than 70 men, women, and children tried to sail to freedom on the *Pearl*. The ship was stopped. Jennings spent years helping to raise money to buy the freedom of two children who were sold after they were captured.

This is the portrait of George Washington that Paul Jennings helped Dolley Madison save. It was painted by Gilbert Stuart.

Paul wrote about his memories of the British attack on Washington in *A Colored Man's Reminiscences of James Madison*, which was published in 1865. Dolley Madison and French John told their own versions of the story. This book combines the memories of all three.

Once he was free, Paul Jennings worked for the government, at the Department of the Interior. He lived in Washington until his death in 1874.

Bibliography

Altoff, Gerard T. *Amongst My Best Men: African-Americans and the War of 1812.* Put-in-Bay, OH: Perry Group, 1996.

Arnett, Ethel Stephens. *Mrs. James Madison: The Incomparable Dolley.* Greensboro, NC: Piedmont Press, 1972.

Jennings, Paul. *A Colored Man's Reminiscences of James Madison.* Brooklyn: Beadle, 1865.

Klapthor, Margaret Brown. "Benjamin Latrobe and Dolley Madison Decorate the White House, 1809–1811." *Contributions from the Museum of History and Technology,* 49 (1966).

Madison, Dolley. Papers. Library of Congress, Washington, DC.

Madison, James. Papers. Library of Congress, Washington, DC.

McCormick, John H. "The First Master of Ceremonies of the White House." *Records of the Columbia Historical Society* 7 (1904).

Pitch, Anthony S. *The Burning of Washington.* Annapolis, MD: Naval Institute Press, 1998.

White House History, no. 1 (1983).

White House History, no. 4 (1998).